CENGAGE Learning

Novels for Students, Volume 20

Project Editors: Ira Mark Milne and Timothy Sisler **Editorial**: Anne Marie Hacht, Maikue Vang

Rights Acquisition and Management: Edna Hedblad, Sheila Spencer, Ann Taylor **Manufacturing**: Rhonda Williams

Imaging: Lezlie Light, Mike Logusz, Kelly A. Quin **Product Design**: Pamela A. E. Galbreath

Product Manager: Meggin Condino

For more information, contact
Thomson Gale
27500 Drake Rd.
Farmington Hills, MI 48331-3535
Or you can visit our Internet site at

corrected in future editions.

ISBN 0-7876-6943-1
ISSN 1094-3552

Printed in the United States of America
10 9 8 7 6 5 4 3 2 1

The Picture of Dorian Gray

Oscar Wilde

1891

Introduction

Oscar Wilde's *The Picture of Dorian Gray* was published simultaneously in Philadelphia's *Lippincott's Monthly Magazine* and by Ward, Lock and Company in England, in July, 1890. In England, the novella was condemned by many reviewers as shocking and immoral. Wilde tried to address some of these criticisms as he worked on an expanded version of the story, which was published as a full-length novel in 1891, along with a preface in which Wilde stated his artistic credo.

The novel centers on Dorian Gray, a young man of great beauty. When he meets Lord Henry Wotton, Lord Henry inspires him with a vision of life in which the pursuit of beauty through sensual pleasure is valued above ethical or moral concerns. Another friend of Dorian, the artist Basil Hallward, awakens Dorian's vanity. After admiring a portrait of himself painted by Basil, Dorian declares that he would give his own soul if he could remain eternally young while the portrait grows old. He gets his wish, and the picture shows the gradual disfigurement of his soul as he sinks into a life of degradation and crime.

As a variation on the Faust legend, with echoes of the fall of man and the Adonis myth, and as an examination of the relationship between art and life, *The Picture of Dorian Gray* fascinated readers into the early 2000s and gave rise to many different interpretations.

Author Biography

Irish poet, novelist, and playwright Oscar Fingal O'Flahertie Wills Wilde was born on October 16, 1854, the son of Sir William Wilde, a distinguished doctor, and Jane Francesca Elgee, a poet and journalist. Wilde attended the Portora Royal School at Enniskillen, where he excelled at classics. In 1871, he was awarded the Royal School Scholarship to attend Trinity College in Dublin. He excelled there also, winning the college's Berkeley Gold Medal for Greek and being awarded a Demyship scholarship to Magdalen College in Oxford. At Oxford, Wilde won the Newdigate prize for his poem, "Ravenna," and was awarded a First Class degree in 1878.

After graduation, Wilde moved to London, where he became famous in fashionable and intellectual circles for his witty conversation and outlandish dress. He quickly established himself as one of the leaders of the Aesthetic Movement, and in 1881 he published his first collection of poetry, *Poems*. In January 1882, he began a lecture tour of the United States. On his arrival he famously told customs officers that he had nothing to declare but his genius. During the course of nearly a year, Wilde delivered over 140 lectures on aesthetics.

The following year, Wilde's play *Vera* was produced in New York, and Wilde became engaged to Constance Lloyd, whom he married in 1884.

They had two sons, Cyril in 1885 and Vyvyan in 1886. To support his new family, Wilde became editor of *The Woman's World* magazine, from 1887 to 1889.

Wilde then embarked on the most creative period of his life. In 1888, he published a collection of children's stories, *"The Happy Prince" and Other Tales*. In 1890, *The Picture of Dorian Gray*, Wilde's only novel, was published in serial form in an American magazine. The following year it was expanded and published in book form. In 1892, another collection of children's stories, *The House of Pomegranates*, appeared.

Wilde then wrote a series of highly successful plays. The first of these society comedies was *Lady Windermere's Fan* (1892), followed by *A Woman of No Importance* (1893), *An Ideal Husband* (1895), and *The Importance of Being Earnest* (1895), all of which were highly acclaimed by public and critics alike. But *Salomé*, a poetic drama Wilde wrote in French in 1891, was refused a license by the Lord Chamberlain. It was never produced in England in Wilde's lifetime.

In 1895, the series of events that was to lead to Wilde's downfall began. Since 1891, he had been

close friends with Lord Alfred Douglas, and Douglas's father, the Marquis of Queensberry, now accused him of homosexuality. Wilde responded by suing the marquis for criminal libel. The marquis was acquitted, but Wilde was arrested and convicted of gross indecency. He was sentenced to two years hard labor. After he was released, he traveled to France and never returned to England. *The Ballad of Reading Gaol* (1898) was a response to his prison experience. Wilde wandered around Europe, staying with friends, until 1900, when he returned to Paris. He died of meningitis on November 30, 1900.

Plot Summary

Chapters 1–5

The Picture of Dorian Gray begins on an afternoon in London, in the studio of the artist Basil Hallward. Basil discusses his latest portrait, of an extremely handsome young man named Dorian Gray, with Lord Henry Wotton. Basil says he will not exhibit the painting because he has put too much of himself in it. After they go into the garden, Basil explains how captivated he has been by Dorian since he first met him a couple of months earlier. Lord Henry makes some witty, cynical remarks about life, and Basil chides him that he does not really believe what he is saying. Then Basil expands on how Dorian's personality has suggested to him an entirely new manner in art; he sees and thinks differently now and envisions a new school of art, in which soul and body are in perfect harmony.

They return to the house, where Dorian is waiting. Basil puts the finishing touches to his painting as Lord Henry expounds his philosophy of how to live a full life, which is not to be afraid of passion and sensuality as a way to fulfillment of the soul. Dorian is moved by Henry's words, and Henry goes on to speak of the beauty of youth and how it is destroyed by time. When Dorian looks at the finished portrait of himself, he is struck by his own beauty in a way he has never felt before. He feels sad that he will grow old and his beauty will be spoiled. He then says he would give everything, even his own soul, if he could always remain young, and the picture grow old instead.

A month later, Dorian informs Henry that he has fallen in love with a young actress named Sibyl Vane, who plays Shakespearean roles in a tawdry theater in the London back streets. Henry regards this attachment as an interesting psychological phenomenon, and he resolves to study the nature of Dorian's sudden passion. Later, he receives a telegram from Dorian announcing that he is engaged to marry Sibyl.

Sibyl explains to her mother about her love for Dorian, whom she calls Prince Charming. Her mother thinks she is too young to fall in love. James Vane, Sibyl's sixteen-year-old brother, who is about to leave for Australia, is concerned for her welfare. He is suspicious of Prince Charming and tells his sister that if the man ever wrongs her, he will kill him.

Chapters 6–10

Dorian, Henry, and Basil go to see Sibyl play Juliet in *Romeo and Juliet*. Her performance is awful, and Henry and Basil leave after the second act. After the performance, Sibyl admits to Dorian that she acted poorly. She explains that now she is in love with him, she knows what real love is, and all the dramatic roles she has acted seem unreal. She can no longer believe in them. But Dorian says he only loves her because she is able to bring great art to life, and he does not wish to see her again. When he goes home he notices the picture of himself has changed. There is an expression of cruelty in the smile. He hides the picture behind a screen and resolves to go back to Sibyl, make amends, and marry her.

The following afternoon, Lord Henry brings him the news that Sibyl is dead. Henry makes some cynical remarks about love and encourages Dorian to view Sibyl's death as resembling a scene from a play. Dorian quickly overcomes his grief and vows to enjoy remaining young. He convinces himself he does not care what happens to the picture.

The next morning, Basil reproaches Dorian for his callousness and attributes it to the influence of Lord Henry. Dorian says he can never sit for him again and refuses to allow Basil to look at the picture he painted. Basil wants to exhibit it, but he reluctantly accepts Dorian's decision. Dorian arranges for the picture to be hidden away in an upper room that has not been used for years.

Chapters 11–15

As the years go by, rumors circulate in London about Dorian's lifestyle, but his charming appearance makes it hard for anyone to think ill of him. The picture, however, grows more horrible, as he continually searches for new sensations and frequents disreputable areas of London. People start to distrust him. There are whispers of scandals.

Media Adaptations

- *The Picture of Dorian Gray* has been adapted to film in the following versions: the version starring George Sanders (Warner, 1945); the version directed by Glenn Jordan (1973); and the BBC version, directed by John Gorrie, with Sir John Gielgud as Lord Henry (1976).

When he is thirty-eight years old, he meets Basil by chance in a London street. He has not seen the artist for a long time. Dorian invites Basil into his house, where Basil confronts him with the stories about how he has ruined so many people's reputations. Scandal follows him everywhere. Basil wonders whether he really knows Dorian and remarks that to find out, he would have to see his soul. Dorian says he will show Basil his soul, and he takes the bemused artist to the room where the picture is stored. He removes the curtain that covers the picture and shows it to Basil, who is horrified. Dorian feels a rush of hatred for the artist and stabs him with a knife, killing him. He goes downstairs to the library and ponders how he can get away with his crime.

The next day he summons Alan Campbell, who used to be his close friend, to his house. Campbell is an expert in chemistry, with a reputation for undertaking unusual experiments. Dorian tells Campbell that he has murdered a man and asks him to destroy the body so that no trace of it remains. Campbell refuses until Dorian threatens to blackmail him over some shameful secret that Dorian knows about him.

That night, after attending a dinner party, Dorian burns Basil's coat and bag. At midnight he goes out and hires a hansom cab.

Chapters 16–19

Dorian is taken to an opium den in a disreputable part of the city. There he encounters Adrian Singleton, one of his former friends who has been disgraced. As he leaves, a woman yells at him, calling him Prince Charming. A sailor hears this and follows Dorian outside. The sailor is James Vane, who accosts Dorian and intends to kill him. But when the still-youthful-looking Dorian points out that whoever deserted Sibyl must be many years older than he, Vane lets him go. But then the woman who called Dorian Prince Charming tells Vane that she first encountered him eighteen years earlier. Vane rushes after Dorian, intending to kill him, but Dorian has vanished.

A week later, Dorian is attending a dinner party when he thinks he sees Vane peering in at the window. He fears for his life and does not go out for three days. Then he joins a shooting-party led by Sir Geoffrey Clouston, the brother of the Duchess of Monmouth. The hunt is called off after Sir Geoffrey accidentally shoots and kills a man. The man turns out to be James Vane.

Dorian now bitterly regrets his life and desires to change. He tries to do good by breaking off a relationship with a working-class girl named Hetty, whom he has been deceiving. But Lord Henry mocks his desire to change, saying he is perfect as he is. Later, tormented by his corrupt life, Dorian takes a knife and slashes the picture. The servants then hear a terrible cry. Dorian is discovered dead, with a knife in his heart, but the picture is as perfect as the day it was painted, and shows Dorian in all his youthful beauty.

Characters

Alan Campbell

Alan Campbell is a former close friend of Dorian Gray. The friendship lasted for eighteen months and ended for unknown reasons. After the split between the two men, Campbell became melancholy and gave up playing music, which had been his delight. After he murders Basil, Gray summons Campbell, who is an expert in chemistry, to dispose of the body. Campbell agrees to do it only after Gray indicates he will blackmail him if he does not cooperate. Campbell later commits suicide by shooting himself in his laboratory.

Lord Fermor

Lord Fermor is the uncle of Lord Henry Wotton. He is a bachelor and former diplomat who devotes himself to what the narrator describes as "the great aristocratic art of doing absolutely nothing." He informs Lord Henry about Dorian Gray's family background.

Dorian Gray

Dorian Gray is twenty years old when the novel begins. He is the grandson of Lord Kelso, and his mother was the beautiful Lady Margaret

Devereux. Margaret married a man Lord Kelso did not approve of, and her father arranged for the man to be killed in a duel. Dorian's mother died within a year, and Dorian was raised by his grandfather. When Dorian comes of age at twenty-one, he will inherit enough money to enable him to live comfortably.

Dorian possesses great physical beauty, and the artist Basil Hallward is infatuated with him. When Dorian meets Lord Henry Wotton, he falls under the influence of Henry's new hedonism, in which the goal of immediate sensual pleasure is valued above ethics or morality. Soon after Dorian meets Lord Henry he falls in love with the actress Sibyl Vane but rejects her when she declares that since she has fallen in love with him, she no longer cares for creating art. It is Dorian's callous response to Sibyl's resulting suicide that produces the first change in the portrait that Basil painted of him: a distinctly cruel expression appears on the face. After this, Dorian pursues a life of pleasure in which he courts all manner of sensual enjoyments, searching for beauty in fleeting sensations and objects of art.

But since he does not balance his love of beauty with a sense of morality, he sinks into selfish behavior. He leads many of his friends to ruin or disgrace, and as the years go by, rumors circulate in London about his objectionable behavior, and people start to shun him. In his physical appearance, however, he remains as youthful as the day the portrait was painted. The degradation of his soul is registered only in the picture.

Dorian sinks to his lowest point when he murders his friend Basil, who has made the mistake of inquiring too closely into the nature of his activities. Dorian effectively covers up his crime, and when James Vane, who has been trying to kill him, is killed in a hunting accident, it appears that Dorian is safe. But he is weighed down by his dissolute life and desires to change it, a goal for which he receives no encouragement from his friend Lord Henry. Eventually, driven to desperation, Dorian slashes the picture on which his sins are visible, but in a mysterious act of transference, Dorian himself dies of a knife wound through his heart, and the picture is restored to its original condition.

Basil Hallward

Basil Hallward is an artist who paints the picture of Dorian Gray. He is completely captivated by the beautiful Dorian, whom he has known for two months, and paints him in many different guises. He secretly worships Dorian and later confesses this adoration to him. He believes that Dorian has inspired him to create the best work of his life. Through Dorian he has discovered a new style of painting and hopes it will be the beginning of a new school that will combine the best of the Greek and Romantic spirit, presenting a harmony of spirit and passion, body and soul. Basil does not intend to exhibit the painting because he says he has put too much of himself into it. Instead, he presents it to Dorian.

Unlike his friend Lord Henry, whose cynicism he regards as a mere pose, Basil does not take an amoral approach to life. He tries to console Dorian after the death of Sibyl Vane and is shocked by the callousness of his friend. He attributes Dorian's attitude to the bad influence of Lord Henry.

After this exchange, Basil and Dorian meet seldom. Eighteen years after their first meeting, they run into each other by chance. Basil demands to know from Dorian the truth regarding the many rumors about Dorian's bad behavior. Dorian resents his criticism. He decides to show Basil the real state of his soul, which is revealed in the picture. Basil only has time to express his horror at the alteration in the picture before Dorian stabs him to death with a knife. Since Basil had been due to depart for Paris that same night and planned to remain there for six months, he is not missed for some time.

Adrian Singleton

Adrian Singleton is a former friend of Gray's. Dorian encounters him again at the opium den, and it is clear that Singleton has been disgraced as a result of his association with Dorian. None of his friends will speak to him, and he takes refuge in an opium addiction.

James Vane

James Vane is the sixteen-year-old brother of Sibyl Vane. He becomes a sailor, but not before he has vowed that if Sibyl's aristocratic admirer, whom he knows only by the name of Prince Charming, ever wrongs her, he will kill him. Eighteen years later, he spots Dorian Gray in an opium den, follows him out to the street, and is ready to kill him, but Dorian convinces him that he has got the wrong man. Vane soon realizes his mistake, and eventually tracks Dorian down, but he is accidentally shot and killed when he intrudes on a hunting expedition.

Mrs. Vane

Mrs. Vane is the mother of Sibyl and James Vane. Like her daughter, she is an actress, but she is a tired woman who has had a hard life. The family lives in poverty because Mrs. Vane was not married to the father of her children, and he died without making provision for them.

Sibyl Vane

Sibyl Vane is a seventeen-year-old girl who excels as an actress. She performs many of the great Shakespearean roles in a tawdry theater in the back streets of London. Dorian Gray falls in love with her, and she with him. But he rejects her after she performs badly, and she is so distressed by his rejection she commits suicide.

Lord Henry Wotton

Lord Henry Wotton, an aristocratic man of

thirty, is a friend of Basil Hallward. He has a languid manner and smokes cigarettes constantly. He is married, but later his wife runs away with another man. When he meets Dorian Gray, he makes such an impression on the younger man that Dorian tries to put into practice the kind of life that he thinks Lord Henry espouses. Lord Henry, however, although he advocates the pursuit of sensual experience for its own sake, tries to remain a spectator of life. Although he and Dorian become friends, he watches Dorian's life as if he is observing a psychological experiment conducted by himself. He is amoral and cynical in his attitudes and expresses no sympathy after the death of Sibyl Vane or the disappearance of Basil. Lord Henry likes to apply his keen intelligence to making epigrams at dinner parties or in conversation with Basil and Dorian. He seems to prefer coming up with witty sayings that reverse conventional notions or morality than getting involved in the realities of life. Basil sometimes says that Lord Henry does not really believe a word he says. Late in the novel, Lord Henry does admit that he would like to be young again, but typically, he immediately takes refuge in a witticism that effectively disguises his real feelings: "To get back my youth I would do anything in the world, except take exercise, get up early, or be respectable."

Homoerotic Love

Although the theme of homoerotic love is never stated explicitly (and could not be, given the conventions of the day), it may be present in Basil's feelings for Dorian. He tells Lord Henry that he cannot he happy if he does not see Dorian every day. He is upset when Dorian becomes engaged to Sibyl. Later, he confesses to Dorian that from the first moment they met, he worshipped him. He says, "I grew jealous of every one to whom you spoke. I wanted to have you all to myself. I was only happy when I was with you." He is completely dominated by his feelings for the younger man, which also transfigure his perception of the entire world. Everything becomes wonderful to him because of Dorian. Basil presents what may be homoerotic attraction in different terms, as the lure of an aesthetic ideal. He worships Dorian because the beautiful young man allows him to fulfill his highest ideals as an artist. He tells Lord Henry that Dorian is to him "simply a motive in art."

The Indulgence of the Senses

Dorian attempts to live according to the view of life presented to him by Lord Henry. Lord Henry believes that nothing is gained by self-denial. He tells Dorian that people should not be afraid of their own desires and impulses, because in them lie the seeds of fulfillment and joy. His credo is "to cure the soul by means of the senses, and the senses by means of the soul." To live a full life, it is necessary to savor with the senses every passing moment. It is better to experience everything the world has to offer than to spend time worrying about ethics or morals. It is better to seek beauty, in the contemplation of art and beautiful objects, than to tie up the mind in intellectual concerns and with education. Lord Henry calls this philosophy a "new Hedonism." (Hedonism is defined as pleasure-seeking as a way of life.)

The novel presents at least two different ways of interpreting this theme. Since Dorian, who attempts to follow Lord Henry's advice, ends up destroying many people's lives, committing murder and suicide, and also corrupting his own soul, there is either something intrinsically wrong with Lord Henry's new Hedonism, or Dorian has failed to understand it or erred in the way he has put it into practice.

Topics for Further Study

- Who is most to blame for the tragedy of Dorian Gray—Lord Henry, Basil Hallward, or Dorian himself?

- Research how attitudes toward homosexuality have changed over the last hundred years. How and why did the changes occur? What are the issues facing the United States today regarding homosexuality?

- What is the relationship between art and morality? Should art be moral? Should it serve some social good? Should the government have the right to censure works of art that it finds morally objectionable?

- Imagine that you are Lord Henry

Wotton and write three epigrams of your own. Remember that an epigram is a short, witty saying that works by inverting conventional expectations and sometimes using a paradox to create a surprise effect.

Both views are possible. The novel can be read in moralistic terms as a condemnation of Dorian's self-indulgent life. In a letter to the *Daily Chronicle* on June 30, 1890 (quoted in *The Artist as Critic*), Wilde himself sought to counter charges that the book was immoral and stated that it did have a moral: "All excess, as well as all renunciation, brings its own punishment." Wilde refers not only to Dorian but also to Basil and Lord Henry. Basil (said Wilde) worships physical beauty too much and creates an overweening vanity in Dorian, whereas Lord Henry seeks to be merely a spectator in life and is even more wounded by that stance than are those, like Dorian, who enter into life with more vigor. However, Wilde's explanation is not in keeping with the preface to the novel, which he added after the negative reviews were published. The preface states in a number of different epigrammatic ways that art should have nothing to do with morality.

The second possible interpretation is that Dorian fails to understand Lord Henry's credo. Indeed, it seems that Lord Henry himself does not live according to it either. As Wilde stated, he remains largely a spectator in life. His manner is languid, and he cultivates an ironic detachment from everything, even as he advocates passionate involvement. Lord Henry seems to do very little during the course of the novel other than exert psychological dominance over Dorian and attend dinner parties for the sole purpose of shocking people with his epigrams. But near the end he confides in Dorian: "I have sorrows, Dorian, of my own, that even you know nothing of."

It seems that Lord Henry's ideal is to take exquisite pleasure in the experience of the senses, to be wide awake sensually in every single moment of existence, while at the same time remaining undisturbed, keeping an evenness of mind. This is a paradox, since the proclaimed ideal is to be simultaneously involved and uninvolved in life. Lord Henry's error is to cultivate one ideal—detachment—at the expense of the other. Dorian makes the opposite mistake. Neither is able to fulfill the theoretical goal of the new Hedonism.

Style

Epigram

An epigram is a short, witty statement in prose or verse. Wilde is famous for his epigrams, and the novel furnishes many examples, almost all of them uttered by Lord Henry Wotton. "A man cannot be too careful in the choice of his enemies," he tells his friend Basil. The humorous effect is gained by a reversal of the expected meaning, since it would be natural to expect to hear "friends" instead of "enemies." The reversal creates a comic surprise. Lord Henry uses the same reversal of expectations when he says, "The only way to get rid of a temptation is to yield to it." This can also be described as a paradox, which is a statement that appears to be contradictory or absurd but on examination may prove to be true. Wilde's preface to the novel also contains many epigrams, many of which show his eagerness to undermine conventional ideas, as in "No artist has ethical sympathies. An ethical sympathy in an artist is an unpardonable mannerism of style."

Myth

Underlying the narrative are suggestions of several myths, including the fall of man as described in Genesis. Dorian, as an innocent, beautiful young man, newly created (in a sense) by

Basil Hallward, the artist/God, is the equivalent of Adam in the Garden of Eden before the Fall. Lord Henry Wotton plays the role of Satan. He tempts Dorian with the promise of a fuller, richer life, if he will only follow his, Henry's, credo. Dorian has too much pride and egoism to resist the temptation, and so he falls.

There is also an allusion to the medieval legend of Faust. Faust is a man who sells his soul to the devil in exchange for knowledge and power, just as Dorian makes a bargain to keep his eternal youth even if it means the loss of his soul.

Another allusion is to the classical myth of Narcissus, who falls in love with himself after seeing his reflection in a pool. When Lord Henry first sees the picture he compares Dorian to Narcissus. This gives a clue to the vanity inherent in Dorian's nature. Lord Henry may tempt him, but in a sense he is only drawing out the qualities that are already present in Dorian.

Aestheticism and Decadence

Aestheticism was a literary movement in late nineteenth-century France and Britain. It was a reaction to the notion that all art should have a utilitarian or social value. According to the Aesthetic Movement, art justifies its own existence by expressing and embodying beauty. The slogan of the movement was "art for art's sake," and it contrasted the perfection possible through art with what it regarded as the imperfections of nature and of real life. The artist should not concern himself with political or social issues.

In France, Aestheticism was associated with the work of Charles Baudelaire, Gustave Flaubert, and Stéphane Mallarmé. In England, its chief theorist was Walter Pater (1839–1894), who was a professor of classics at Oxford University. In contrast to the usual Victorian emphasis on work and social responsibility, Pater emphasized the fleeting nature of life and argued that the most important thing was to relish the exquisite sensations life brings, especially those stimulated by a work of art. The aim was to be fully present and to live vividly in each passing moment. As Pater put it in the "Conclusion" to his work *Studies in the History of the Renaissance* (1873), which is in effect a manifesto of the Aesthetic Movement in

England, "To burn always with this hard, gemlike flame, to maintain this ecstasy, is success in life." This is in complete opposition to the prevailing Victorian mentality, with its emphasis on hard work, moral earnestness, and material success.

Wilde was an admirer of Pater, and it was Wilde who later became the representative figure of Aestheticism. Pater's influence on *The Picture of Dorian Gray* was profound. When Dorian adopts Lord Henry's belief that the aim of the new Hedonism "was to be experience itself, and not the fruits of experience" he is virtually quoting Pater's "Conclusion," in which he writes, "Not the fruit of experience, but experience itself, is the end."

Pater was a key figure in the emergence of the later movement in England and France known as Decadence. This movement flourished in the last two decades of the nineteenth century, a period also known as fin de siècle (end of the century). Decadent writers believed that Western civilization was in a condition of decay, and they attacked the accepted moral and ethical standards of the day. The theory of Decadence was that all "natural" forms and behaviors were inherently flawed; therefore, highly artificial, "unnatural" forms and styles were to be cultivated, in life as well as art. Many Decadent writers therefore experimented with lifestyles that involved drugs and depravity (just as Dorian does in *The Picture of Dorian Gray*).

One influential work of the Decadent movement was *À Rebours* (*Against the Grain*), a novel by French writer, J. K. Huysmans, published in 1884. The protagonist is estranged from Parisian society and continually seeks out strange and new experiences. It is generally accepted that *À Rebours* is the novel that Lord Henry sends to Dorian Gray and which fascinates and grips Dorian for years.

Compare & Contrast

- **1890s:** Male homosexuality is a crime in England, punishable by imprisonment.
  Today: Homosexuality is no longer a crime. In law, homosexual people are treated the same as everyone else. However, many people holding conservative and religious views based on the Bible still regard homosexuality as a sin.

- **1890s:** Britain is the foremost power in the world but faces increasing rivalry from the growing industrial and military strength of Germany.
  Today: Britain and Germany, having fought against each other in two world wars, are now allies within the European Community and NATO. Britain is no longer the leading power in the world.

- **1890s:** Class divisions are emphatic in Britain, and there is a wide contrast in dress, manners, and way of life between those who are comfortably off and those who are poor. Families are large. Only working class women take employment outside the home. University education is not available for women of any class or for the working classes.

Today: Britain is a more egalitarian society than at any time in its history. The influence of mass culture, through television, films, and advertising, has tended to erode differences between classes in dress and manners. Women of all classes now make up a large percentage of the workforce, and higher education is open to all.

Another example of Decadent literature is Wilde's play *Salomé*, with its lurid subject and imagery of blood, sex, and death. In addition to Wilde, Decadence in England was associated with the poets Algernon Swinburne and Ernest Dowson, and the painter, Aubrey Beardsley.

Critical Overview

When first published in England, *The Picture of Dorian Gray* met with a storm of negative reviews, many of which attacked the book in virulent terms for its alleged immorality. The *Daily Chronicle*, for example, assailed its "effeminate frivolity, its studied insincerity, its theatrical cynicism, its tawdry mysticism, its flippant philosophisings and the contaminating trail of garish vulgarity" (quoted in Norbert Kohl's *Oscar Wilde: The Works of a Conformist Rebel*). The anonymous critic for the *St. James's Gazette* affected a manner of even greater disgust when he wrote, "not wishing to offend the nostrils of decent persons, we do not propose to analyse [the novel] … that would be to advertise the developments of an esoteric prurience" (quoted in Michael Patrick Gillespie's "*The Picture of Dorian Gray*: What the World Thinks Me"). This critic even ventured the opinion that he would be pleased to see Wilde or his publishers prosecuted for publishing the novel.

In letters to the editor of the *St. James's Gazette*, Wilde defended himself against such charges. He insisted that *The Picture of Dorian Gray* had a very clear moral and that his main problem in writing the book had been to keep the obvious moral from subverting the artistic effect.

Although not all early reviews were unfavorable, the negative impression created by those who denounced the book affected how people responded to it for decades. Passages from the novel were read in court by the prosecution during Wilde's trial for homosexuality in 1895. The habit of interpreting the novel, and other works by Wilde, in the context of his life dominated early scholarship about Wilde. Some twentieth-century and twenty-first-century critics continued to use biographical details to shed light on *The Picture of Dorian Gray*; others examined it in relation to the cultural context in which it was written or used archetypal criticism, in which the novel was analyzed in terms of myths and legends such as the Faust story. Some critics interpreted the novel by examining issues of sexual orientation.

What Do I Read Next?

- *The Importance of Being Earnest* (1895; first published, 1899) was the last of Wilde's four stage comedies and is generally regarded as his masterpiece. It sparkles with that unique Wildean wit. Wilde's aim in writing it was to treat the trivial things in life seriously and the serious things with triviality.

- Richard Ellmann's biography *Oscar Wilde* (1987) is indispensable for the study of Wilde's life. Ellmann presents Wilde as the tragic hero of his own life.

- *Dorian: [An Imitation]* (2004), by British novelist Will Self, is a retelling of *The Picture of Dorian Gray* set in the last two decades of the twentieth century. All the same characters appear. Henry Wotton is a gay heroin addict, "Baz" Hallward is a video artist, and the narcissistic Dorian Gray is a seducer of both men and women. By 1997, all three are HIV-positive, but Dorian shows no sign of illness.

- *Oscar Wilde: Myths, Miracles and Imitations* (1996), by John Stokes, shows how Wilde played a vital part in the development of modern culture. Stokes examines diaries, letters, dramatizations of Wilde's plays, and impersonations of the man himself, and discusses Wilde's relationship to fin-de-siècle and twentieth century ideas.

Sources

Ericksen, Donald H., *Oscar Wilde*, Twayne's English Authors Series, No. 211, Twayne Publishers, 1977, pp. 96–117.

Gillespie, Michael Patrick, *The Picture of Dorian Gray: "What the World Thinks Me,"* Twayne's Masterwork Studies, No. 145, Twayne Publishers, 1995.

Kohl, Norbert, *Oscar Wilde: The Works of a Conformist Rebel*, translated by David Henry Wilson, Cambridge University Press, 1989, p. 138.

Pater, Walter, "Conclusion," in *The Norton Anthology of English Literature*, 4th ed., Vol. 2, Norton, 1979, pp. 1580–83, originally published in *Studies in the History of the Renaissance*, 1873.

Wilde, Oscar, "The Critic as Artist," in *The Artist as Critic: Critical Writings of Oscar Wilde*, edited by Richard Ellmann, Random House, 1969, pp. 340–408.

——, *The Picture of Dorian Gray*, Unicorn Press, 1948.

Further Reading

Cohen, Ed, "Writing Gone Wilde: Homoerotic Desire in the Closet of Representation," in *Critical Essays on Oscar Wilde*, edited by Regenia Gagnier, G. K. Hall, 1991, pp. 68–87.

> Cohen analyzes *The Picture of Dorian Gray* to show how even in the absence of explicit homosexual terminology or activity, a text can subvert the traditional standards and representations of appropriate male behavior.

Cohen, Philip K., *The Moral Vision of Oscar Wilde*, Fair-leigh Dickinson University Press, 1978, pp. 105–55.

> Cohen argues that Wilde's recurrent themes are sin and salvation and a conflict between the moral perspectives of Old and New Testament, judgment and love. He explores these themes in *The Picture of Dorian Gray*.

Paglia, Camille, *Sexual Personae: Art and Decadence from Nefertiti to Emily Dickinson*, Vintage, 1991, pp. 512–30.

> As part of her celebrated, controversial, and wide-ranging examination of Western culture,

Paglia treats *The Picture of Dorian Gray* as the fullest study of the Decadent erotic principle: the transformation of person into *objet d'art*.

Raby, Peter, *Oscar Wilde*, Cambridge University Press, 1988, pp. 67–80.

This is an introductory essay that emphasizes two major elements in the novel: the Sybil Vane episode and the yellow book that Lord Henry sends Dorian.

Lightning Source UK Ltd.
Milton Keynes UK
UKHW02f2142030818
326744UK00004B/229/P